WINDOWS 11 MANUAL FOR SENIORS

A Beginners Guide to Navigate Your Computer with Step-by-Step Instructions

LARRY WELLS

Contents

PREFACE

People of all ages can use Windows 11 with confidence after reading this book. Windows 11 is Microsoft's newest operating system. This guide will give you easy-to-follow steps and tips to make your computer experience better, whether you are new to computers or moving up from an older version of Windows.

How to Follow This Guide

This guide is set up to walk you through different parts of Windows 11 one step at a time. From how to turn on your computer for the first time to how to use the internet, each chapter focuses on a different topic. To make learning as easy as possible, we've added photos, tips, and real-life examples. You can read the book from beginning to end or skip to certain parts if you need to.

1

Getting Started

1.1 A Look at Windows 11

The newest operating system from Microsoft is called Windows 11. It is meant to be easy for everyone to use, even older people. Windows 11 aims to make using your computer fun and useful by giving you a better and sleeker design, more security features, and a lot of useful tools. That's because this guidebook will walk you through every important part of this operating system, making sure you understand how it works.

Even though it might seem hard to get started with a new operating system, don't worry—this guide was made with beginners in mind. It will be easy for you to follow along and learn the system as we go because we will break everything down into simple two-step steps.

1.2 Needs for Hardware

To make sure you have a smooth experience with Windows 11, you should make sure your computer meets the hardware needs. For Windows 11, you need a 64-bit processor that works with it, at least 4 gigabytes (GB) of RAM, and at least 64 GB of storage space. It should also have a display with a resolution of 720p or higher and a graphics card that works with DirectX 12.

If you're not sure if your computer meets these standards or if you need help, don't be afraid to ask a computer expert. They can help you figure out if you need to upgrade any hardware.

1.3 Getting Your Computer Ready

Before you begin, make sure that your computer is turned on by pressing the power button. Bear with us while Windows 11 loads. It might take a while. It will show you the lock screen when the operating system is fully loaded. After this, you'll need to use a password, PIN, or some other way of authentication that you have set up to log in to your computer.

1.4 Moving Around on the Desktop

Once you've signed in, you'll be taken to the Windows 11 desktop, which is where you'll do most of your work. Icons and a taskbar on the screen make it easy to get to different features and programs. For a more personalized look, you can change the desktop to fit your tastes.

In the bottom left corner of the screen, on the desktop, you'll find the Start button. When you click on it, the Start screen will appear. From there, you can get to all of your programs, settings, and files.

1.5 How to Use the Taskbar

The taskbar, which is at the bottom of the screen, makes it easy to get to important features and open programs. It has the Start button and the system tray, which shows icons for services like the clock, Wi-Fi, and music control. The taskbar also shows all of your open programs as separate buttons, which makes it easy to switch between them.

1. 6 Turning Off Your Computer

There are two ways to turn off your computer: click the "Start" button and choose "Power" followed by "Shut down," or press the power button on your computer and choose "Shut down" from the menu that appears. It's important to shut down your computer correctly so that you don't lose info or damage it.

You've done a great job of starting to use Windows 11. We talked about the basic ideas that will help you use your computer more easily in this chapter. The next part will go into more detail about the Windows 11 user interface and all of its features and settings.

Windows 11 is a big improvement over the versions that came before it. It makes things easier to use and more organized. With a new taskbar, a simplified Start menu, and better window control tools, it's easy to use. Let's go over some basic ideas first before getting into these parts.

The Desktop: When your computer starts up, the desktop is the first thing you'll see. It is the main area of the screen where you can get to files, programs, and links.

The Start Menu: It's at the bottom left of your screen and lets you get to everything on your computer. It's where your apps, settings, and power choices are kept.

The Taskbar is the bar at the bottom of your screen that lets you quickly get to open programs, the Start menu, and system information.

Putting and taking away your computer

Press the power button, which is generally on the front or side of your computer, to turn it on. When you turn on Windows 11, it will walk you through setting it up for the first time. Click the "Start" button, then click the "Power" icon, and finally click "Shut down."

Taskbar: In Windows 11, the taskbar is more than just a row of items. It's a flexible tool that lets you quickly switch between open apps, see the time and date, get system messages, and get to important settings. You can change how it looks and feel, so you can pin your favorite apps for quick access.

Action Center: The Action Center is on the right side of the taskbar and is where alerts and quick settings are kept. This is where you'll find system messages, alerts from apps, and quick links to important settings like Wi-Fi, Bluetooth, and lighting.

How to Turn Your Computer On and Off (Part 2)

When you turn on your Windows 11 computer for the first time, it will go through a setup process. To do this, you need to connect to Wi-Fi, make an account, and pick your personal settings. Microsoft gives you step-by-step instructions to make this process easy.

The safest way to shut down your computer is through the Start menu. To turn off your computer, press the "Start" button, then click on the "Power" icon. This makes sure that all of your programs are properly stopped so that any updates or installations can finish.

Getting signed in and setting up your account

You'll be asked to sign in the first time you turn on your computer. You can use a Microsoft account, which syncs your settings and preferences across all of your Windows devices, or you can make a private account that is only used on this computer.

Making changes to basic settings

If you're already logged in, you might want to check out the Settings app. Here is where you can change the settings on your computer to make it work the way you want it to. From the Start menu, you can get to Settings. System lets you change settings for your screen and sound, Devices lets you handle connected devices like printers and mice, and Personalization lets you change your desktop background and taskbar layout.

How to Connect to the Internet

It's easy to connect to the internet on Windows 11. Then pick out your network and enter the password. To do this, click on the Wi-Fi button in the taskbar. Plug in the Ethernet cable if you're using a wired link, and Windows should connect itself.

Changes to Windows 11

It is very important to keep your Windows 11 up to date for protection and performance reasons. Windows usually checks for changes on its own, but you can do it yourself by going to Settings > Update & Security > Windows Update.

2

Navigating the Windows Interface

We will look at the Windows 11 interface and learn how to easily get around on your computer in this part. Learning how to use the different parts of the Windows system will help you feel more at ease and confident when you use your computer. Okay, let's begin!

1. The Start Menu: The Start menu is one of the most important parts of the Windows 11 design. The Start menu is in the bottom left area of your screen. It lets you quickly get to your favorite apps, documents, and settings. Just click on the

Windows icon or press the Windows key on your computer to get to the Start menu.

2. Taskbar: The taskbar is at the bottom of your screen and makes it easy to get to programs you use often. Along the taskbar are icons or buttons that show which programs are open. This makes it easy to switch between them. You can also change how the taskbar looks by saving frequently used apps or removing ones that aren't needed.

3. Task View: Task View is a new tool in Windows 11 that lets you keep track of all of your open windows and virtual desktops. You can see all of your open windows in a virtual area by clicking on the Task View icon on the taskbar. It looks like two rectangles that overlap. This feature comes in handy when you have a lot of work to do or need to clean up your screen.

4. Action Center: To get to the Action Center, click on the warning icon in the upper right corner

of the taskbar. It gives you quick access to a number of system settings and alerts. As a primary hub, it lets you manage notifications, change the brightness, turn on or off features, and more. Take the time to look through the Action Center's different settings to make your Windows experience more unique.

5. File Explorer: You'll use File Explorer, which is shown by a folder icon on the taskbar, to move between your files and folders. If you click on this icon, a window with your file structure will appear. You can search for files and folders, sort them, copy them, move them, and delete them here. You can't do without File Explorer if you want to organize your photos, videos, papers, and other computer files.

6. Search: Windows 11 has a powerful and improved search function that lets you find files, apps, settings, and even web results fast. Clicking on the search icon on the taskbar, next to the Start button, will take you to the search feature. Just

type in your search term, and Windows will show you results right away.

These are some of the most important parts of the Windows 11 layout that will make it easier for you to use your computer. You should take your time to look at each feature and get used to how they work. As you get more used to Windows 11, you'll find that its design is easy to understand and use.

Looking Around the Desktop

It's where you'll spend most of your time in Windows 11. This is the screen that shows up when there are no windows open. You can store things here, make folders, and keep quick-access links to your favorite programs here. There are a few important parts to the desktop:

Icons are small pictures that show what your files, folders, and programs are. To open these buttons, double-click on them.

With Task View, you can see all of your open windows and virtual screens. A button on the desktop lets you get to it.

The "Recycle Bin" is where deleted files go before they are erased from your computer for good. You can get files back from the recycle bin or empty it to make room.

How to Use the Start Menu

In Windows 11, the Start menu has been changed to make it simpler and easier to use. When you click the Windows button in the middle of your taskbar, it opens. Inside you'll find these things:

Pinned Apps: You can pin your most-used apps here to make them easy to get to.

All Apps: This is a list of all the programs that are on your computer.

Power button: This button turns off your computer, starts it up again, or puts it to sleep.

How to Use the Taskbar

In Windows 11, the taskbar is at the bottom of the screen. All the things you need are easy to find there:

Search: To look for files, apps, or information on the web, click this link.

Widgets: This new tool lets you get to news, weather, and other data quickly.

Windows Store and Your Apps: The Windows Store and your most-used apps are easy to get to.

It has an action center and notifications.

The Action Center is a key part of staying up to date and managing your settings. It is on the right side of the taskbar, and clicking on the button for it will open it. You'll find the following inside:

Notifications are alerts that your system and apps send you.

Quick Settings: Turn on and off Wi-Fi and Bluetooth, change the lighting, and more.

Calendar: A small clock and calendar for quick use.

3

Managing Files and Folders

We will learn the basics of how to organize files and folders on a Windows 11 computer in this lesson. To use a computer efficiently, you need to know how to make files and folders, organize them, look for them, and take care of them. You should be able to easily find your way around your computer's file system by the end of this chapter.

Part 1: Getting to Know File Explorer

1.1 How to open File Explorer:

Find the File Explorer button in the Start menu or on the taskbar.

- To quickly open File Explorer, press the Windows key + E on your computer.

1.2 How to Use the File Explorer Window:

– Moving around in the menu, the toolbar, the navigation pane, and the file preview pane.

– Changing the views in File Explorer to fit your tastes.

Part 2: Making and Managing Folders

1.11 Making a New Folder:

- Right-clicking in the area you want to create a new folder in and choosing "New Folder."

- Naming the area correctly and knowing how important it is to pick names that mean something.

2.2 Putting Folders and Subfolders in Order:

– Moving files around in File Explorer by dragging and dropping them.

- Putting your things in even more order by creating subfolders.

Part 3: Making and Organizing Files

3.1 Adding New Files:

— Opening the place you want to find in File Explorer.

: Right-click and pick "New" to pick the type of file you want to make (for example, Word document, Excel worksheet).

3.2 Saving Files: - Figure out how to use "Save As" and what the file name and type should be.

- Picking a good place to save things so they are easy to get to.

3.3 Changing File Names:

– Pressing "Right-click" on a file and picking "Rename."

- Putting in a new name that says what it is and hitting "Enter" to save the changes.

3.4 Getting rid of and restoring files:

- Choose the file(s) you want to get rid of and press the Delete key.

— Learning about the Recycle Bin and how to get back things that you accidentally deleted.

Part 4: Looking for Folders and Files

4.1 How to Use the Search Bar:

– Finding the search bar in the window for File Explorer.

– Typing words or sentences to look for certain folders or files.

4.2 Customizing Search Filters: - Know the different search filters that are available, such as by file type or date last changed.

– Using filters to get better search results and find things faster.

Making folders and putting them away

It's important to organize your files and groups so that they are easy to find and use. You can make files on your desktop or in the File Explorer in Windows 11.

To make a new folder, right-click on the desktop or in File Explorer and choose "New." Then, choose "Folder." Give it a name that goes with it.

To move files, you can either drag and drop them into groups or use the right-click menu to "Cut" and "Paste."

Organizing Folders: Use folders to group things that are similar together. For example, put all of your pictures in a folder called "Pictures."

Trying to Find Files

The Windows search tool makes it easy to find things. You can search in File Explorer, the Start menu, or the desktop.

How to Use the Search Bar: Type the file's name or a word into the form.

Filters: You can narrow your search by type, date, and other factors by using filters.

How to Copy, Cut, Paste, and Delete Files

To manage your files, you need to know how to do these simple things:

Copy and Paste: This lets you make copies of files or folders. To copy something, right-click on it and choose "Copy." Then, right-click where you want the copy to go and choose "Paste."

When you cut and paste, the thing goes to a different place. Right-click, pick "Cut," and then pick "Paste" in the new spot.

Right-click on a file or folder and choose "Delete" to get rid of it. This sends it to the Recycle Bin, but you can get it back if you need to.

How to Use External Storage Devices

It's easy to connect external storage devices like USB sticks. When you connect them, they will show up in File Explorer, where you can handle files just like on your computer's hard drive.

4

Customizing Your Experience

This part will talk about the different ways you can change Windows 11 to make it work the way you want it to. This chapter will show you step-by-step how to customize your computer so that you can have a truly unique and enjoyable experience. It will cover everything from making your screen your own to changing your accessibility settings.

Part 1: Making your desktop your own

1.1 Picking a Background for Your Desktop:

   - To begin, right-click on an empty spot on your screen and choose "Personalize" from the menu that appears.

2. In the box for personalization, click on the "Background" tab on the left.

The third step is to look through the pictures and choose the one you want. You can also pick a single color or a slideshow of pictures.

- Step 4: Close the window and enjoy your new desktop background after making your choice.

1.2 Changing the background of the lock screen:

Step 1: To change how the lock screen looks, go to the window called "Personalization" as we talked about before.

- Step 2: On the left, click the "Lock screen" tab.

- Step 3: To make your lock screen look better, you can pick a background picture, a photo video, or even a Windows Spotlight.

- Step 4: Choose the option you want and close the window. When your computer is locked, you'll now see the background you picked.

Part 2: Taking care of the Start menu and taskbar

2.1 Setting up your Start Menu:

- To get to the Start Menu, press the "Start" button.

- Step 2: To change the size of the start menu, move your mouse over its sides until the resize cursor shows up. Then, click and drag to make the menu the size you want.

- Step 3: To pin an app to the Start Menu, find it in the Apps List, right-click on it, and choose "Pin to Start."

Step 4: Click and drag your pinned apps and files to where you want them on the Start Menu to arrange them.

- Step 5: Right-click on an app or folder that you want to remove from the start menu and choose "Unpin from Start."

2.2 Making Changes to the Taskbar:

- Step 1: Right-click on an empty spot on the taskbar and choose "Taskbar settings" from the menu that appears.

- Step 2: Change different settings in the Taskbar settings window, like how the Taskbar is aligned, whether it is hidden or shown, and whether the system buttons are enabled or disabled.

3. To pin frequently used apps to the taskbar, just drag and drop them from the Apps List to where you want them on the Taskbar.

Step 4: Click and drag the saved apps to where you want them to be in the list to change their order.

- Right-click on an app that is pinned and choose "Unpin from taskbar."

Part 3: Changing the settings for accessibility

3.1 Improving access for the visually impaired:

- To get to the Settings app, press the Start button and choose "Settings."

Second, find "Accessibility" in the list on the left and click on it.

- Step 3: Try out different visual settings, like word size, high contrast, and magnifier, to make your computer easier to use.

—Step 4: Made the changes you want, and then closed the Accessibility settings when you were done.

3.2 Making it easier for people to hear:

- Step 1: Open the Settings app and choose "Accessibility" as we talked about earlier.

- Step 2: Change settings like closed captions, audio changes, or visual alerts under "Audio" to help people who have trouble hearing.

—Step 3: Make the changes you need to make based on your wants and preferences, then close the settings for accessibility.

Your computer will really feel like yours if you make changes to how Windows 11 works for you. This chapter gave you the information you need to make your computer fit your needs. You can now customize the desktop and lock screen, set up the Start Menu and taskbar, and change the accessibility settings. Spend some time looking into these customization choices. They will make your Windows 11 experience more enjoyable and tailored to your needs.

Making changes to the desktop and taskbar

You can make your computer feel more like you and be easier to use by changing the way the screen and taskbar look and work.

To change the background of your screen, right-click it and select "Personalize." You can choose a background from this list or add your own picture.

To change the settings for the taskbar, right-click on it and choose "Taskbar settings." You can move the taskbar around, pick which items show up, and do other things.

Changing the system settings

In Windows 11, the "Settings" app is where you can make changes to how your computer works.

System Settings lets you change the brightness of the screen, the volume of the sound, and the alerts.

Device Settings: Take care of things like printers, keyboards, and mice that are linked.

Network & Internet: Set up your network links, such as Wi-Fi.

Setting up features for accessibility

Windows 11 has a lot of features that make computers easy for people of all skill levels to use.

That's right, this tool can zoom in on parts of your screen to make text and pictures easier to see.

A screen-reading app reads the words on the screen out loud.

Closed Captions: You can change how closed captions show up in movies.

Changing the privacy settings

You can choose what information your computer shares and collects by changing the privacy settings.

How to Track Your position: Choose which apps can use your position.

The camera and the mic Privacy: You can control which apps can use your microphone and camera.

5

Using Basic Applications

1. Getting to Know the Start Menu: The Start Menu is where you can access all of Windows 11's apps and functions. You can find it in the bottom left part of your screen. It is easy to open; just press the Windows key or click on the Start button. Open the Start Menu. On the left is a list of commonly used programs. On the right is a grid of installed programs that you can change. Take some time to look through this menu and get used to how it's set up.

2. When you use the Microsoft Edge browser:

The web browser that comes with Windows 11 is Microsoft Edge. You can use it to surf the web, look for information, and talk to other people. Go to the Start Menu and look for Microsoft Edge. You can also click on the Edge icon in the taskbar. When the address bar is open, you can type a website URL or a search term and press Enter to go to a page. Spend some time getting used to using bookmarks, tabs, and other tools on different websites.

3. Getting to Know the Mail App:

The Mail app makes it easy to manage all of your email accounts from one place. Look for "Mail" in the Start Menu to open it. If you don't already have an email account, add yours by following the steps shown on the screen. Once everything is set up, it's easy to write, share, receive, and organize emails. You should take some time to get used to the Mail app's interface and functions.

4. Figuring out how to use the calendar:

The Calendar app is a must-have for keeping track of your events, meetings, and schedule. In the Start Menu, look for "Calendar" to open it. When you open the Calendar app, you'll see a monthly view with different events marked on different dates. The calendar can be synced with other devices and new events can be added. Explore the Calendar app for a while and make some practice events to get a feel for how it works.

5. How to Use the Microsoft Store:

The Microsoft Store is where you can get a lot of different programs and apps for your Windows 11 computer. Find the Microsoft Store button in the taskbar and click on it to open it. You can also search for "Microsoft Store" in the Start Menu. Once it's open, you can look through different types of apps, find specific ones, and install them with just one click. Take some time to look around the Microsoft Store and find apps that fit your wants and interests.

Remember that these are just a few of the basic programs that you can use on your Windows 11 computer. After you get used to these apps, you can try out other ones that come with your phone, like Photos, Groove Music, and Microsoft Office Suite. Take your time with each app to get used to its design and features.

A Look at Some Common Applications

Windows 11 has many built-in programs that can be used for everyday tasks and needs. Here are some of the most important apps:

WordPad is a simple program for editing text that works well for making notes or letters.

Calculator: This tool can do more than just simple math. It has modes for programming, science, and even drawing.

Photos: Look at, change, and arrange your picture files.

Calendar: Keep track of your plans and meetings.

Making use of the web browser

Microsoft Edge, the browser that comes with Windows 11, lets you browse the web safely and quickly.

To move around on the internet, type a URL or search term into the address bar.

With bookmarks, you can easily get to your favorite websites.

Privacy and security: Edge has tools that protect your privacy online, such as the ability to stop tracking.

How to Use Email

It's important to stay in touch through email. The Mail app in Windows 11 lets you write and receive emails and keep them in order.

Setting Up Email Accounts: You can add more than one email account from different sources.

Writing and Sending Emails: Learn how to write emails, send them, and attach files.

Taking Care of Your Inbox: Use folders and flags to sort and manage your emails.

6

Security and Maintenance

It is more important than ever to keep your computer safe in this modern world. This chapter will show you the most important care and safety steps you need to take to keep your Windows 11 computer safe and running well. If you follow these step-by-step instructions, you'll be able to handle the complicated world of computer security with ease and keep your device running smoothly for years to come.

Part 1: Keeping your computer safe

1.1 Setting up accounts for users:

– Making sure your Microsoft account password is safe

– Knowing why user accounts are important and what they do for computer security

– Adding more user accounts and controlling how much access they have

1.2 Security Features in Windows:

– Learning about the Windows Security app and what it can do

– Turning on and setting up Windows Defender Antivirus

– Setting up Windows Firewall to protect the network

– Managing and setting up Windows Security changes

– Making use of Windows Hello for easier and better login

1.3 Safety While Browsing the Web:

– Setting up and installing a good antivirus program

- Making Windows Defender SmartScreen work to stop fake attacks

– Learning how to use and understand the security features of the Microsoft Edge browser

- How to browse safely to stay away from dangerous websites and downloads

Part 2: Maintenance and Improvement

2.1 Cleanup and management of disk space:

- Cleaning up your computer regularly to make room comes free

– Managing disk space automatically with Storage Sense

– Effectively managing storage options and personal files

– Learning about and using the cloud storage choices in OneDrive

Updates and patches for Windows 2.2:

– Making changes to Windows Update

– Knowing how important it is to keep your system updated

– Making sure your computer has the most recent security fixes and feature updates

- Taking care of optional changes and installing drivers

2.3 Getting the Best Performance:

– Keeping an eye on and improving system speed with the Task Manager

- Taking care of startup apps to make boot times faster

— Improving the performance of visual effects

- Updating drivers to make gear work better with newer versions of Windows

This chapter taught you how to keep your Windows 11 system safe and running at its best through regular maintenance and security checks. By following the step-by-step steps here, you can keep your computer safe from threats and make sure it works at its best. Remember that the best way to keep your computer safe and running smoothly is to update security features and do maintenance tasks on a regular basis.

Basic Rules for Safety

When you use a computer, especially one that is linked to the internet, security is very important. Here are some basic things you can do to keep your Windows 11 computer safe:

Making Strong Passwords: For your passwords, use a mix of letters, numbers, and special characters.

Windows Security is a built-in tool that protects your computer with an antivirus program, sets up a firewall, and more.

Watch out for phishing and scams: learn to spot emails and websites that seem fishy. Don't click on links or download attachments from sites you don't know or trust.

Keeping your computer up to date

For safety and usefulness, regular updates are necessary:

Windows Update: This tool gets and installs Windows updates for you immediately. Settings > Update & Security lets you check for changes by hand.

Keeping your device drivers up to date is important for getting the best results.

Making user accounts and managing them

Making different user accounts is a good idea if more than one person uses your computer: To add new users, open the Settings app and go to Accounts > Family & other users.

Setting Permissions: You can give different users and groups different amounts of access and permissions for each account.

Keeping copies of your data

Your info can be saved from loss if you back it up regularly:

File History: This tool lets you back up your files automatically to a network location or an external drive.

Setting up System Restore Points: If something goes wrong, you can use restore points to get your machine back to a previous state.

7

Accessibility Features

Technology has become an important part of our lives because it helps us stay in touch with friends and family, get information, and get things done faster. However, older people may have trouble with some devices and apps because they are too complicated. Luckily, Windows 11 comes with a number of built-in accessibility tools that make it easier for seniors to use their computers. We will talk about these features and how they can make your computer experience better in this chapter.

Easy to Get to Center:

Microsoft has merged the Ease of Access Center so that Windows 11 can be used by people of all ages and skill levels. You can customize and change different accessibility settings to fit your needs from this central hub. Click on Start, then Settings, and finally Accessibility to get to the Ease of Access Center.

2. Spaces for displays:

Windows 11 has a number of tools that can make the screen better for older people. Changing the size of text, icons, and other visual features can make things a lot easier to read. To change these settings, go to the Ease of Access Center and click on the Display tab. Then, try out the different choices until you find the one that works best for you.

3. A loupe:

The Magnifier tool can help you a lot if you have trouble reading small text or making out small details on your computer screen. You can make content bigger and zoom in on certain areas to make them stand out more with this tool. Press the Windows logo key and the plus sign (+) at the same time to turn on Magnifier. After that, you can make the settings just right for your wants.

4: The Narrator:

The Narrator tool can be very helpful for people who have trouble seeing. This screen-reading tool lets your computer read out loud the words on your screen, so people who are blind or have low vision can use it. Press the Windows logo key and the Control key (Ctrl) at the same time to start Narrator. From there, you can try out the different Narrator choices to make the reading experience fit your needs.

5. Recognition of speech:

If you have trouble using a keyboard and mouse to type or move around, Windows 11 has a speech recognition tool built in. For easy handling of your computer, you can use voice commands. Press the Windows logo key and the letter H at the same time to turn on speech recognition. Make sure the microphone you're connecting to your computer works, and then follow the on-screen steps to set up the feature.

6. Captions that are closed:

Captions are very important for people who have trouble hearing because they help them understand what is being said. There are closed captioning options in Windows 11 that can be changed to show captions for different videos and programs. In the Ease of Access Center, go to the Captions tab to change these options.

7. Being able to use a keyboard:

There are a lot of keyboard shortcuts and disability settings in Windows 11 that can help you get around your computer faster. Sticky Keys, for instance, let you press one key at a time, which is helpful for people whose fingers don't move very easily. Filter Keys ignores short or repeated typing, which helps people whose hands shake or aren't steady make fewer mistakes. You can change these settings and find more keyboard options by going to the Keyboard tab in the Ease of Access Center.

No matter what age or skill level you have, using your computer shouldn't be hard. Windows 11 has many accessibility features that are meant to help seniors use their computers successfully and on their own. You can customize your computer experience and get around any problems by using these built-in tools. Take the time to learn about the settings and change them to fit your needs. Also, keep in mind that technology can be a part of your life that brings people together and gives you power.

A Look at the Accessibility Options

Windows 11 is made to be accessible, with a lot of tools that can help people with different needs.

Here are a few of the most important traits for accessibility:

You can zoom in on parts of your screen with this tool, which makes text and pictures easier to see.

Narrator: A screen reader reads the words on your screen out loud, which helps people who have trouble seeing.

High Contrast Mode: This mode makes the color contrast between text and pictures on your screen stronger, so you can tell them apart better.

Changing the settings for accessibility

Changing these settings can make your computer experience much better:

In the Settings app, you can find the Ease of Access Center. This is where you can change all of your accessibility settings to suit your needs.

Keyboard Shortcuts: To get to these features fast, learn how to use these shortcuts.

Speech Recognition: You can use your voice to control your PC and dictate text with this tool.

How to Use Video Closed Captions

Closed captions can be very helpful for people who have trouble hearing:

Turning on Closed Captions: Find out how to make closed captions work in video apps and change how they look.

Alerts that you can see and hear

These features can help people who have trouble hearing:

Visual Notifications: Use visual cues instead of or in addition to sound messages.

Sound Alerts: Change how sound alerts sound to make them stand out more.

8

Troubleshooting Common Issues

This chapter will talk about some of the most common problems seniors may have with Windows 11 and give them step-by-step directions on how to fix them. Whether your computer is running slowly, has software bugs, or is having trouble connecting, this chapter will help you quickly fix these problems. When you follow the steps in this chapter, you'll become better at fixing problems and enjoy Windows 11 more generally.

Part 1: Slow Performance

Slow performance is a regular problem with Windows 11 that can make you less productive and less happy with it overall. To fix this problem, we will now show you some steps to take right now.

1. Look at the system requirements. Make sure your computer meets the Windows 11 basic system requirements. It is important to have enough memory, storage, and processing speed to get the best performance.

2. Close any programs that you don't need. Having a lot of programs running at once can slow down your computer. To free up resources and speed things up, close any background apps that you don't need to use.

3. Get rid of startup items you don't need. Some programs are set to run immediately when you turn on your computer, which slows it down. To turn off startup things that aren't needed, do these steps:

a. To open the Task Manager, press Ctrl + Shift + Esc.

Be sure to click on the "Startup" tab.

c. Pick out the apps you want to turn off and click "Disable" in the bottom right corner.

4. Get rid of temporary files. These files can build up over time and take up important storage space, which could slow down your computer. Click on these links to get rid of temporary files:

a. To open the Run box, press the Windows key + R.

b. Type "%temp%" and press "Enter."

c. To delete all the files in the temporary folder for good, select them all and press Shift + Delete.

Part 2: Bugs in the software

It's annoying when software bugs happen, but they don't have to be hard to fix. In this article, we'll talk about some common program problems and give you steps to fix them.

1. Repair Windows 11: Keeping up with the latest updates for Windows 11 can help fix program bugs. To make your machine new:

a. Hit the Windows key.

b. Open the "Settings" app.

c. From the list on the left, choose "Windows Update."

d. Click "Check for updates" and then do what it says on the screen.

2. Use the Windows Troubleshooter. Windows 11 has a built-in troubleshooter that can find and fix common issues instantly. To make it work:

a. Hit the Windows key.

b. Open the "Settings" app.

4. Choose "System" from the list on the left.

d. Click on "Troubleshoot" and pick the area that fits your problem, like "Hardware and Devices" or "Windows Update."

3. restart software that is giving you trouble: If a certain program is giving you trouble, you might want to restart it. How to do it:

a. Hit the Windows key.

b. Open the "Settings" app.

3. Choose "Apps" from the list on the left.

d. Find the program that is giving you trouble and click on it.

e. Click "Uninstall" and check out the steps shown on the screen.

f. Get the most recent version of the program from the website and run it again.

Part 3: Problems with Connectivity

Problems with the internet, printers, and other gadgets are common and can make you less productive. This part will be about troubleshooting steps to fix issues with connection.

1. Check your network connections. Make sure you can join to your network and that your internet connection is stable. It might help to restart your computer and router.

2. Use the Network Troubleshooter. Windows 11 has a Network Troubleshooter that can instantly find and fix problems with networks. To get to it, do these things:

a. In the menu, click on the network icon, which is usually in the bottom right corner.

b. From the choice that appears, choose "Troubleshoot problems."

c. Do what the troubleshooter tells you to do on the screen.

3. Reinstall device drivers: Problems with connection can happen when device drivers are out of date or broken. To put device drivers back on:

1. Press the Windows key and X together, then choose "Device Manager" from the list that comes up.

b. Figure out which gadget is making it hard to connect.

c. Select the device with the right mouse button and click "Uninstall device."

d. Restart your computer, and Windows will load the right drivers again on its own.

By following the steps in this chapter for debugging, you can fix common problems that happen when you use Windows 11. Remember that the best ways to fix problems are to practice and be patient. If you need more help, don't be afraid to ask for it, and keep looking into what Linux has to offer with Windows 11. Once you know how to fix problems, you'll be able to confidently use your computer.

Basic Methods for Fixing Problems

Systems can have problems even if they are very stable. Here are some easy steps you can take to fix common Windows 11 issues:

Restarting Your Computer: Restarting your computer can often fix a lot of problems.

Getting Updates: Make sure that Windows 11 is up to date. Updates can fix bugs and make the system run better.

Running the Troubleshooter: Windows 11 has a number of troubleshooters that can fix common issues instantly. Setting > Update & Security > Troubleshoot is where you can find these.

How to Deal with Slow Performance

Follow these steps if your computer is moving slowly:

Closing apps you don't need: If you have too many open, your computer may run more slowly.

Disk Cleanup: This tool helps you make more room on your hard drive, which can make it run faster.

Taking Care of Startup Programs: When you turn on your computer, some programs run immediately. You can speed up the boot time by turning off startup apps that you don't need.

Fixing Problems with Internet Connectivity

Having trouble with the internet can be annoying. Here are some ways to fix them:

Restarting your modem or router: If something is wrong, it might not be your computer but your internet link.

Network Troubleshooter: This built-in tool can help you figure out what's wrong with your network and fix it.

When to Ask for Extra Help

If you've tried simple fixes and are still having problems, it may be time to get help from a professional:

Support: Get in touch with Microsoft Support or a reputable computer repair business.

Looking for answers on online forums: Sites like the Microsoft Community can help you find answers to common issues.

9

Quick Tricks and Tips

Quick tips and tricks are in a special section.

Tips and quick tricks you can use every day

Here are some quick and useful tips that will make your time with Windows 11 better:

Cuts on the keyboard:

Press Ctrl + C to copy, Ctrl + V to paste, and Ctrl + X to cut.

To switch between open apps, press Alt + Tab.

Press Windows + D to show or hide the desktop.

To take a screenshot, press Windows + Shift + S. To take a screenshot of the whole screen, press PrtScn.

Using Snap Layouts: To see snap layouts, move your mouse over the expand button on any window. This will let you better arrange your windows.

Voice Typing: Press Windows + H to start voice typing, which is useful for dictate text instead of typing it.

Quickly Finding Files: Press Windows + S to bring up the search bar. This will help you quickly find files, settings, or apps.

Special Part: Frequently Asked Questions

Questions People Ask Often

This part answers some of the most common questions and worries people have about Windows 11:

How do I get new programs to run on my computer?

Answer: You can get new apps from the Microsoft Store, which has a lot of them, or from places you know you can trust.

What should I do if my computer stops working?

A: To end any programs that won't work, press Ctrl + Alt + Delete and choose "Task Manager." If that doesn't work, you might need to restart.

How can I make the words bigger so it's easier to read?

A: To change the size of the word, go to Settings > Ease of Access > Display.

Q: Can I back up my files with a portable hard drive?

A: Yes, a great way to back up your files is to connect an external hard drive and use the File History option.

How do I make sure my computer is safe?

A: Use strong passwords, stay away from sketchy emails and websites, and keep your system up to date. Also, use Windows Security features.

www.ingramcontent.com/pod-product-compliance
Ingram Content Group UK Ltd.
Pitfield, Milton Keynes, MK11 3LW, UK
UKHW020647070725
6747UKWH00059B/401

9 798223 329015